HISTORY OF BRITAIN

VICTORIAN BRITAIN

1837 to 1901

Revised and updated

Andrew Langley

Heinemann
LIBRARY

www.heinemann.co.uk/library
Visit our website to find out more information about Heinemann Library books.

To order:
☎ Phone 44 (0) 1865 888112
📄 Send a fax to 44 (0) 1865 314091
💻 Visit the Heinemann bookshop at www.heinemann.co.uk/library to browse our catalogue and order online.

First published in Great Britain by Heinemann Library, Halley Court, Jordan Hill, Oxford OX2 8EJ, part of Harcourt Education.
Heinemann is a registered trademark of Harcourt Education Ltd.

© Harcourt Education Ltd 1994, 2006
The moral right of the proprietor has been asserted.

Editorial: Lionel Bender and Richard Woodham
Design: Ben White and Michelle Lisseter
Picture Research: Jennie Karrach and Mica Brancic
Production: Helen McCreath

Originated by RMW
Printed and bound in China by WKT Company Limited

10 digit ISBN 0 431 10815 3
13 digit ISBN 978 0 431 10815 5
10 09 08 07 06
10 9 8 7 6 5 4 3 2 1

British Library Cataloguing in Publication Data
Langley, Andrew
Victorian Britain. – 2nd ed. – (History of Britain)
941'.081
A full catalogue record for this book is available from the British Library.

Acknowledgements
The publishers would like to thank the following for permission to reproduce photographs:
Page 6 (left): Lionheart Books; page 6 (right): The Royal Collection 1993 Her Majesty Queen Elizabeth II; page 7: Peter Newark's Historical Pictures; page 8: National Waterways Museum, Gloucester; page 9 (top): The Mansell Collection; page 9 (bottom): Fotomas Index; page 10, page 11 (left): The Bridgeman Art Library; page 11 (right): The Mansell Collection; page 12/13: The Royal Collection 1993 Her Majesty Queen Elizabeth II; page 12 (top): Gunnersbury Park Museum; page 13: The Royal Library, Windsor Castle; page 15: Lionheart Books; page 16/17: Cossack Bay by Roger Fenton/The Royal Photographic Society; page 18: The Mansell Collection; page 20: Lionheart Books; page 21 (top): The Mansell Collection; page 21 (bottom): Hulton Deutsch Collection; page 23: Board of the Trustees of the Victoria and Albert Museum; page 24 (top): The Mansell Collection; page 24 (bottom): Gunnersbury Park Museum; page 26 (left): The Mansell Collection; page 26 (right): Hulton Deutsch Collection; page 27: Lionheart Books; page 28 (all): Gunnersbury Park Museum; page 29, 30: The Mansell Collection; page 31: The National Trust Photographic Library; page 33, 34 (both): Lionheart Books; page 35: Robert Opie; page 36: National Library of Ireland; page 37, 39: The Mansell Collection; page 40/41: e.t. archive; page 41 (bottom): The Mansell Collection; page 42: e.t. archive; page 43: The Mansell Collection.

Illustrations by Mark Bergin: 10/11, 36/37, 40/41; James Field: 8/9, 12/13, 16/17, 18/19, 26/27, 28/29, 34/35, 38/39, 46; John James: 6/7, 14/15, 20/21, 22/23, 24/25, 30/31, 32/33, 42/43; Malcolm Smythe: page 45.

Cover picture of Queen Victoria in her robes of state (lithograph by Eyre and Spotiswoode from painting by Franz Winterhalter), reproduced with permission of Art Archive.

Every effort has been made to contact copyright holders of any material reproduced in this book. Any omissions will be rectified in subsequent printings if notice is given to the publishers.

The paper used to print this book comes from sustainable resources.

CONTENTS

ABOUT THIS BOOK 4

MAP OF BRITAIN 4

INTRODUCTION 5

THE YOUNG PRINCESS 6

FACTORIES AND TOWNS 8

THE POWER OF STEAM 10

VICTORIA BECOMES QUEEN 12

THE GROWTH OF TRADE 14

TROUBLES ABROAD 16

CHURCH AND CHAPEL 18

SOCIAL REFORM 20

FAMILY LIFE 22

IN THE SUBURBS 24

COUNTRY LIFE...26

EDUCATION 28

PASTIMES 30

MEDICINE AND SCIENCE 32

WORKSHOP OF THE WORLD............................34

THE IRISH PROBLEM 36

EXPLORERS AND MISSIONARIES 38

THE BRITISH EMPIRE......................................40

END OF AN ERA 42

FAMOUS PEOPLE OF VICTORIAN TIMES 44

ROYAL VICTORIANS FAMILY TREE 45

GLOSSARY 46

FIND OUT MORE 47

INDEX...48

*Unfamiliar words are explained in the **glossary** on page 46*

ABOUT THIS BOOK

This book considers the Victorians chronologically, meaning that events are described in the order in which they happened, from 1837 to 1901. Some of the double-page articles deal with a particular part of Victorian history. Those that deal with aspects of everyday life, such as trade, houses, and pastimes, are more general and cover the whole period. Unfamiliar words are explained in the glossary on page 46.

▼ **This map** shows the location of places mentioned in the text. Some are major cities, towns, or the sites of famous buildings or events.

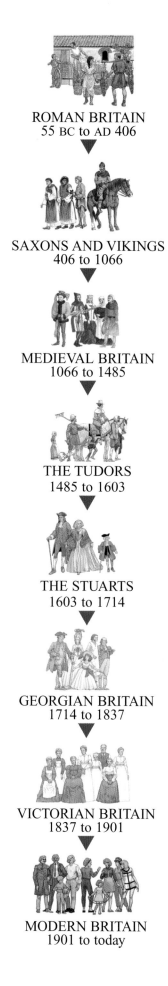

ROMAN BRITAIN
55 BC to AD 406

SAXONS AND VIKINGS
406 to 1066

MEDIEVAL BRITAIN
1066 to 1485

THE TUDORS
1485 to 1603

THE STUARTS
1603 to 1714

GEORGIAN BRITAIN
1714 to 1837

VICTORIAN BRITAIN
1837 to 1901

MODERN BRITAIN
1901 to today

INTRODUCTION

Queen Victoria came to the throne in 1837. She reigned for over 63 years, until 1901 – longer than any other British monarch. During this time, Britain became the richest and most powerful nation in the world.

But the Victorian Age had a difficult beginning. The monarchy was very unpopular after the reigns of the wasteful George IV and the elderly William IV. There were violent riots by factory and farm workers, who wanted better wages and conditions. Some thought that Britain was close to revolution.

It was also an age of reform, or change. A series of Reform Acts gave thousands more people the right to vote for Members of Parliament in elections. Other new laws stopped young children from working in factories and mines, and made them attend school until the age of 13. Cleaner drinking water, sewers, and better hospitals helped protect people from deadly diseases such as cholera and typhus.

The lands controlled by Britain grew into an empire which stretched from Canada in the west to New Zealand in the east. It covered nearly a fifth of the world's land area. Goods from the countries of the empire poured into Britain, to be sold on to other countries at a huge profit. More wealth came from industry. New machines, new factories, and new methods turned out a huge variety of new products. People flocked from the countryside to find work in the rapidly growing factory towns. Steam trains made travel quicker and cheaper than ever.

THE YOUNG PRINCESS

"The Country is very desolate everywhere; there are coals about, and the grass is quite blasted and black... Everywhere, smoking and burning coal heaps, intermingled with wretched huts and carts and ragged children." Princess Victoria wrote this in her diary in August 1832, during a tour of the English Midlands.

Victoria was born on 24 May 1819. She had a lonely and unhappy childhood. Her father died when she was only a few months old. Her uncle, King William IV, had no children, and Victoria would inherit the throne when he died. So her mother kept a close watch on her. Victoria rarely went out.

The young princess met few other children. Her only friend was her stern German governess, Baroness Lehzen. Victoria grew up to be stubborn and quick-tempered, but also dignified and truthful. When told she would be the next monarch, she replied, "I will be good".

▽ **A painting of the young Victoria in 1830.** As a teenager, she was plain in looks. But she was taught to move gracefully. She even had a sprig of holly tied under her chin to make her hold up her head. The princess loved parties, but was rarely allowed to meet boys of her own age.

△ **Kensington Palace and its gardens in London**, where Victoria was born in 1819. Although it was a grand house, the furniture was plain and the carpets worn. Meals were dull, and a cup of tea was "a great treat". Victoria disliked palaces for the rest of her life.

Between 1832 and 1835, Victoria was sent on a series of coach journeys through Britain. Her mother believed that she should see the country she would one day be ruling. The princess travelled to North Wales, the Midlands, Yorkshire, the south coast, and East Anglia. She stayed in hotels, or grand houses such as Chatsworth and Alton Towers (then a private house). Wherever she went, she was greeted with banners, speeches, and concerts in her honour. She described what she saw in a diary.

It was her first sight of the way poor people lived in Britain. She did not know that thousands of children, some as young as seven, had to work in mills and factories instead of going to school. Their jobs were in factories, down mines, or out in the city streets. The employers preferred child workers because they could pay them less than adults. A child might earn £10 (£500 at today's value) a year. When she became queen, Victoria was paid £385,000 a year.

△ **Princess Victoria on her journey through the Midlands in 1832.** This was not a holiday, but part of her education. She had already been taught many subjects, including:
- history
- geography
- Latin
- French
- religion
- poetry
- handwriting
- drawing
- the piano
- singing
- dancing.

△ **A chimney sweep.** Small boys were sent up narrow chimneys to clean them. Some chimneys were still hot.

△ **Young children worked in coal mines** for hours in the dark. They opened and shut traps to let wagons through.

△ **A factory worker.** Some children in cotton mills such as this worked for 16 hours a day among dangerous machines.

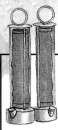

FACTORIES AND TOWNS

Towns were growing rapidly. In 1801, the first census showed that only about one-third of the British population lived in towns. By 1851, this had gone up to a half. Ten cities, including Manchester, Liverpool, and Glasgow, had more than 100,000 inhabitants. Biggest of all was London, with nearly 2,500,000.

△ **A "truck" token.** Some workers were paid with these coins, which could only be spent at the shop run by the company.

People flocked from the countryside to the towns. They came to find work and earn more money. The wages of a farm worker were very low, and there were fewer jobs on the land, thanks mainly to new machines such as threshers. But thousands of new workers were needed to operate machines in mills and foundries. Factory owners built houses for them.

△ **Poor people selling second-hand goods** in the streets of Houndsditch, London, in 1872. One stall has bottles, a violin and a saw. Another has old clothes.

◁▽ **A view of an industrial town in the late 1830s.** The houses and factory buildings are crammed close together. The chimneys of the metal works belch out the smoke from furnaces, filling the air with dust and soot. At the bottom left is the canal which runs beside the works. Boats bring coal and iron from the nearest mines. They also carry the finished goods from the factory all over the country.

▷ **A cartoon** showing a rich man ignoring the poor.

The workers' houses were usually near the factories, so that people could walk to work. They were built as quickly and cheaply as possible. Most houses in the North of England were "back-to-backs", built in double rows. In Scotland, many workers lived in blocks of flats called tenements. The houses were crammed close together, with narrow streets between. Chimneys, bridges, and factory smoke blocked out much of the light.

Almost all these houses were crowded. Five or more people might live in a small single room. Even the cellars were full. In Liverpool in the 1840s, there were 4,400 cellars and nearly 40,000 people living in them.

Most of the new towns were also very dirty and unhealthy. The household rubbish was simply thrown out into the streets. In Manchester in 1832, nearly half of the streets were unpaved and covered in filth, including dung and rotten food. They were an ideal place for germs to breed. More than 31,000 people died during an outbreak of cholera in 1832, and many more were killed by typhus, smallpox, and dysentery.

THE POWER OF STEAM

Many more uses were found for steam power during the early 19th century. The engines built by James Watt in the 1770s had been used to pump water from mines and work machines in factories. Now, inventors developed steam engines which could move along themselves. The railway age had begun.

The first public railway linked the coal mines of Darlington with the port of Stockton. It was built by engineer George Stephenson and opened in 1825. Five years later, he completed another line between Liverpool and Manchester. It was a huge success. By 1835 it was carrying 156,000 tonnes of goods and 470,000 passengers a year.

Railways were not just faster and stronger than other kinds of transport. They were cheaper too. The cost of train travel was about half that of a stage coach. And, for the first time, people could travel more swiftly than a galloping horse. The railways carried food, supplies, and people to the growing factory towns.

More lines were quickly built. In 1841 the Great Western Railway, designed by Isambard Kingdom Brunel, joined London to Bristol. By 1855 there were over 13,000 kilometres of track in Britain.

Many people hated the railways. Farmers and landowners feared that their property would be damaged as new track was laid. Coach and canal owners saw that the railways would put them out of business. Ordinary people were frightened of the speed and the flying sparks from the huge locomotives.

▷ **A Great Western train** comes out of Box Tunnel in Wiltshire. This tunnel was 3 kilometres long (the longest in the world at the time) and took 5 years to dig. Almost all the work of building the railways was done by hand. Armies of men, using only picks, shovels, and barrows, made cuttings and tunnels. These men were called navigators, or navvies for short. Many were from Ireland, where there were few jobs.

▽ **The Railway Station** – a Victorian painting.

△ **Isambard Kingdom Brunel,** one of the greatest Victorian engineers. He built steam ships, such as the *Great Western* (shown above left), and bridges, as well as railways.

▽ **The railway network in the early 1850s.** Between 1844 and 1848 there had been a rush to build new lines. This was called "railway mania". By 1852 all the main routes in Britain had been built.

Glasgow • ● Edinburgh N

Manchester •

Birmingham •

Bristol • ● London

Exeter •

VICTORIA BECOMES QUEEN

"Poor little Queen! She is at an age at which a girl can hardly be trusted to choose a bonnet for herself; yet a task is laid upon her from which an archangel might shrink." Thomas Carlyle wrote this after Victoria's coronation in 1838. When she had come to the throne, the queen was only 18 years old.

King William IV, Victoria's uncle, died on 20 June 1837. Early that morning, the princess was woken up and told that she was Britain's new ruler. At 11:00 a.m., she had her first meeting with her Privy Councillors (chief ministers). She impressed them all with her calmness.

Victoria's closest advisor and friend during the early years of her reign was the Prime Minister, Lord Melbourne. He taught the queen much about politics and government. At the time there were two political parties, the Tories and the Whigs. Melbourne was a Whig.

In 1839, Victoria was visited by her cousin Albert, a German prince. Her family thought that he would make an ideal husband for her, and the queen soon fell in love. The couple were married in February 1840 in London.

At first, many people distrusted the prince because he was a foreigner. But Albert soon became respected for his hard work and his interest in science, the arts, and education. He helped reform the army, and encouraged the building of new museums, including the Natural History Museum in London. The marriage made Victoria very happy. Albert was not just her husband, but also her private secretary.

▷ **Stamp and coins** from Victoria's reign. The Penny Black of 1840 and Penny Red of 1841 were the world's first sticky stamps.

That summer, while the queen was riding in an open carriage from Buckingham Palace, a gunman shot at her twice. She was unharmed, but this was only the first of seven attempts to kill her during her reign. (They all failed.) Victoria showed great courage, and when she next went out to the opera, she was cheered wildly by a large crowd.

The greatest tragedy of Victoria's life struck in 1861, when Albert died of typhoid fever. After this, she seldom went out in public. She wore black mourning clothes and spent much time at remote Balmoral Castle in Scotland.

◁ **The new queen attends her first Privy Council meeting** in Kensington Palace in 1837. This painting shows Lord Melbourne (seated, holding the pen), the Prime Minister, with Lord Palmerston (seated behind him), the Duke of Wellington (standing before the pillar), and Sir Robert Peel (on his left). (Both Palmerston and Peel became Prime Minister later in her reign.) Victoria read out a speech written for her by Lord Melbourne.

▷ **A painting by the queen** of Prince Alfred and Princess Alice. Between 1840 and 1857, Victoria had four sons and five daughters. The eldest son, Albert Edward, became King Edward VII.

△ **Victoria and Prince Albert** after their wedding at St James's Palace. Albert disliked banquets and life in London. He encouraged the queen to spend more time at Windsor Castle and the Isle of Wight.

THE GROWTH OF TRADE

Victoria's reign saw the start of free trade for British farmers and manufacturers. Since Stuart times, Parliament had tried to protect British agriculture and industry from foreign rivals. It had set duties (extra payments) on many goods imported from abroad and had passed Corn Laws to control the import of grain.

Many people believed that this protection harmed British trade, and kept the price of corn too high. An Anti-Corn Law League was formed. In 1846 the Corn Laws were repealed (abolished) by the Conservative Prime Minister Robert Peel. By 1852, duty had been taken away from most goods. Other European countries became free traders too.

Britain swiftly grew to be the world's richest trading nation. Without duty, raw materials such as cotton could be imported more cheaply. At the same time, more factories, mills, and foundries were built. Using new manufacturing processes and steam power, they made machines, textiles, ships, and other goods that were sold overseas.

▽ **Sir Robert Peel** became Tory Prime Minister in 1841. Many Tory MPs were angry when he did away with the Corn Laws, and he was forced to resign. In 1829, Peel had created the first police force in London.

▽ **This chart shows how Britain's trade grew** between 1850 and 1870. More goods were imported than exported. But trades involving services such as banking, rather than goods, brought a great deal of money into the country.

	Imports	Exports	Service trades
1850s	169.5	100.1	101
1860s	260.9	159.7	187
1870s	360.6	218.1	288

(Figures are a yearly average over each decade. They are in £ millions.)

▷ **Building the Crystal Palace in London**, to house the Great Exhibition of 1851. It was designed by Joseph Paxton and made of iron and glass. The iron framework was lifted into place, a section at a time, by two huge cranes. The Palace was 563 metres long and 139 metres wide, and covered an area the size of four football pitches. It was an ideal home for sparrows, which were a nuisance. No-one could find a way to get rid of them, until the Duke of Wellington suggested sparrowhawks. This worked.

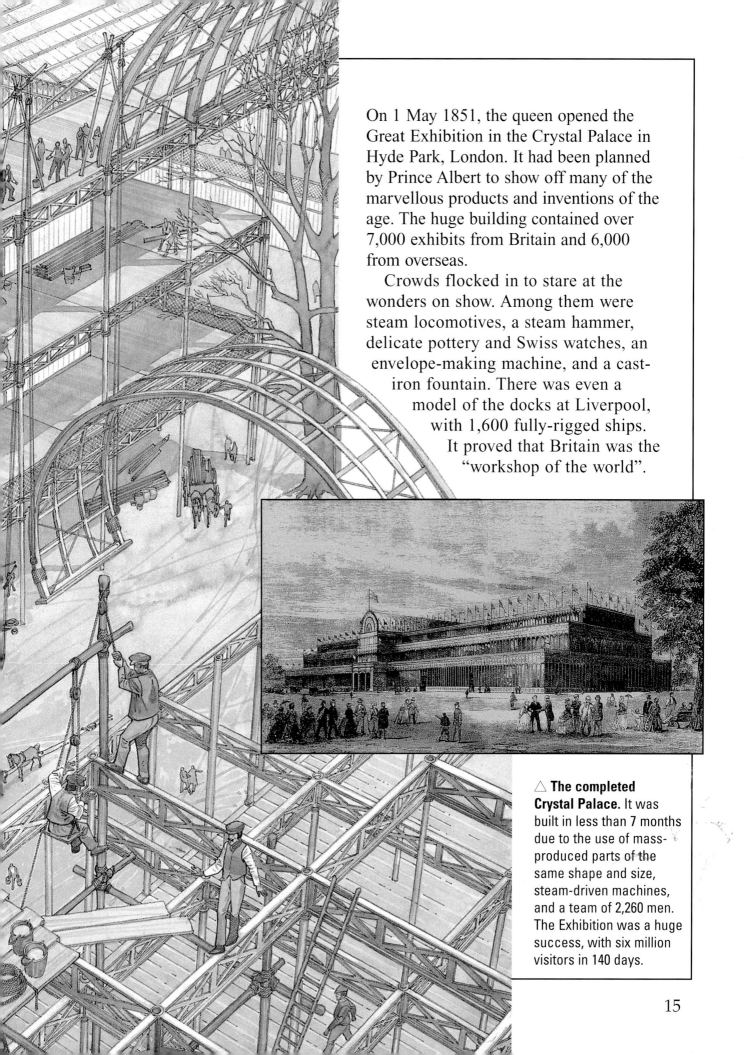

On 1 May 1851, the queen opened the Great Exhibition in the Crystal Palace in Hyde Park, London. It had been planned by Prince Albert to show off many of the marvellous products and inventions of the age. The huge building contained over 7,000 exhibits from Britain and 6,000 from overseas.

Crowds flocked in to stare at the wonders on show. Among them were steam locomotives, a steam hammer, delicate pottery and Swiss watches, an envelope-making machine, and a cast-iron fountain. There was even a model of the docks at Liverpool, with 1,600 fully-rigged ships. It proved that Britain was the "workshop of the world".

△ **The completed Crystal Palace.** It was built in less than 7 months due to the use of mass-produced parts of the same shape and size, steam-driven machines, and a team of 2,260 men. The Exhibition was a huge success, with six million visitors in 140 days.

TROUBLES ABROAD

By 1850, there had been no major war in Europe for 35 years. During this period of peace, Britain's army, although small, had grown strong, and controlled a growing empire. Her navy ruled the ocean from the Atlantic to the China Seas. But in 1853, Turkey declared war on Russia. The Crimean War had begun.

▽ **A map of the Crimea**, an area which juts out from Russia into the Black Sea. The main battles of the war were:
● Alma – a costly victory for the allies
● Balaclava – a Russian attack was driven off
● Inkerman – another Russian attack failed
● Sebastopol – allied guns bombarded the town for 11 months.

RUSSIAN EMPIRE

N

CRIMEA
Alma
Sebastopol •Inkerman
Balaclava
BLACK SEA

△ **Florence Nightingale** went to the Crimea with 38 nurses to care for the wounded. At Scutari Hospital, she soon had 5,000 soldiers to look after, and was working 20 hours a day.

◁ **British soldiers in the Crimea**. Allied and Russian armies suffered badly from icy weather and outbreaks of disease, as well as fierce fighting.

The war was fought between Russia and the allied armies of Britain, France, Turkey, and Sardinia. The allies wanted to stop Russia from seizing territory ruled by Turkey. The allied army of 60,000 men landed in the Crimea in September 1854. It defeated the Russians at Alma and marched on to besiege Sebastopol. The war was to last for over a year.

In October, the Russians made a suprise attack on the British base at Balaclava. During the battle, the British Light Brigade of cavalry charged the main Russian army. The charge was a disaster. Out of 673 men, 247 were killed or wounded.

Winter came, and the allied soldiers had to live in terrible conditions. Few had shelter from the cold, or enough food or medicine. Thousands died from disease or wounds. Sebastopol fell at last in September 1855, and the Russians were forced to make peace in February 1856. Each side had suffered many casualties.

▷ **British troops charge at Indian rebels** in Lucknow in March 1858. There were only 34,000 British soldiers in the Indian army, while there were more than 250,000 Indian troops.

▽ **Photograph of British supply ships** in the harbour at Balaclava.

The Indian Mutiny broke out in 1857. These are some of the causes:
● Indians disliked the way that the British were trying to change their way of life.
● They feared that the British would force them to become Christians.
● All Indian soldiers had to promise that they would fight anywhere in the empire.
● New cartridges were issued to the Indian troops. The cartridges were covered with animal grease – either from pigs (which the Muslims thought unclean) or from cows (which the Hindus thought sacred).
● The setbacks of the Crimean War had shown the Indians that the British were not all-powerful.

Only a year later, the British faced an uprising in India. Three regiments of Indian soldiers mutinied in May 1857. They captured the city of Delhi. The mutiny quickly spread through central India, and hundreds of Europeans were killed. Cawnpore was captured, and rebels surrounded Lucknow. But the mutineers had no proper leader. By early 1858, British troops had driven them out of Delhi and other cities, and killed thousands in a terrible revenge.

CHURCH AND CHAPEL

"Pews for the rich were padded, lined, and cushioned. The poor were seated on stools in the aisles... and the cold, damp stone beneath their feet was the only place to kneel in prayer." This description of an Ipswich church was written in 1850.

The writer is referring to a church belonging to the Church of England, or Anglican Church. This was the established Christian denomination in Britain. Queen Victoria was an Anglican, and so were most rich and middle class people. But few working people went to Anglican churches. They felt out of place, and disliked the hard seats. Worse still, they thought that most parsons were supporters of the landowners. Other kinds of Christians, such as the Methodists and Baptists, had begun by attracting working people. Their services were simple, and held in plain chapels. But by the 1850s most chapel-goers were middle class. The working classes, especially those in the towns, seldom had time to go to church.

▽ **A Sunday service at an Anglican church**. The parson preaches his sermon from the pulpit. It might last for a whole hour. Most middle class families went to church at least once on Sundays. Some went two or three times. Sunday was thought to be "the Lord's Day", and so no work was supposed to be done. Children had to stay at home and read religious books. For working people, Sunday was usually their only day of rest.

▷ **A cartoon of 1861 connected with Charles Darwin**'s theory of evolution. Darwin suggested that humans had evolved from apes. Darwin's most famous book was *The Origin of Species* (1859). This said that the Earth was much older than most people thought, and that animals and plants had evolved over millions of years. Darwin's theory caused an uproar because it disagreed with the story of creation given in the Bible. Many Christians believed that everything in the Bible was true and should not be questioned.

MONKEYANA.

AM. I A MAN AND A BROTHER?

▷ **The Earl of Shaftesbury** and his supporters at a community meeting. He believed it was his duty to God to help the poor. He entered Parliament in 1826, and in the 1830s and 1840s pushed through Parliament a series of Acts to improve the working conditions in factories and coal mines. Later he started "ragged schools" for poor children and 'soup kitchens' where food was given free to the hungry.

△ **Chapels were a focus for social life**, as here at a Methodist chapel in Wales. So too were Methodist schools and public libraries.

In 1851, a census was made in England and Wales of people who went to church on Sundays. It showed that less than half of the population of about 18 million attended a religious service. And only about 5 million of these were members of the Church of England. Church leaders were shocked by these figures, and tried to reform their churches. One group of Anglicans, the Evangelicals, realized that the Church should do more to help the poor in towns. They set up many charities and social clubs in London and industrial cities. Men such as Lord Shaftesbury led campaigns to improve the conditions for people who worked in mines and factories.

The Evangelicals grew into the strongest religious force in Victorian Britain. They believed that all people were sinners, and could only be saved from hell by being sorry for their sins and leading a strict moral life. They held family prayers in their homes. Their missionaries went to Africa and the East to convert people to their faith.

SOCIAL REFORM

As towns and factories grew, so did the problems of the poor. They worked long hours in unhealthy and dangerous mills and mines. Their children had to work too, and not go to school. Bad housing, unclean water, and lack of drains caused deadly diseases.

△ **Improved conditions** in a mental hospital, 1885.

▷ **A metal-working factory in the 1870s.** Two factory inspectors (in top hats) are checking to make sure that the new laws are being obeyed:
● Dangerous machinery, such as drive belts, had to be fenced off.
● No-one had to work for more than 10 hours a day.
● No children could be employed under the age of 10: by 1901, the age had been raised to 12.
● No-one under the age of 18 could work at night.
● All factories and workshops which employed more than five people were to be inspected regularly.

In the 1830s, the Earl of Shaftesbury had begun a great programme of social reform. Slowly, this improved living and working conditions. The Ten-Hour Act of 1847 set a limit to the working day of women and children. Coal mines were inspected regularly to make sure they were safe. In 1874, another Factory Act made it illegal for anyone under 14 to have a full-time job.

Meanwhile, towns were being made more healthy. Edwin Chadwick's report on Public Health in 1842 had shocked the country by showing how bad conditions led to disease. But it was not until 1875 that local authorities were forced to appoint health inspectors and supply cleaner drinking water.

These reforms, together with new hospitals and new ways of treating illness, made people much healthier. In the 1840s, the average life expectancy of a Manchester worker was just 17 years. Rural workers in Wiltshire lived to 33. By the 1880s, a town worker's life expectancy was 30 years, and a country worker's 52 years.

The poor were helped by new laws, and by private charities. Among these were William Booth's Salvation Army, founded in 1878, which gave food and shelter as well as religious teaching.

Social reform covered most of Victorian life:
1853 The end of transportation (sending convicts overseas).
1867 and 1884 Reform Acts allow nearly all men to vote in general elections.
1878 A commission is formed to improve prison conditions like those shown left.

The Army
1871 Officers can no longer buy themselves a rank and must pass exams to get promoted.
1881 Flogging is ended as a punishment.

Women
1870 Wives are allowed to keep any money they earn or inherit.
1888 Some women are allowed to vote in county council elections.

Housing
1875 Local authorities are allowed to pull down slum areas of housing.

▽ **Model farm buildings** and workshops in Wiltshire.

FAMILY LIFE

Families were an important part of Victorian life. Many of them were large. In 1870, the average family had five or six children. Most upper and middle class families lived in large and comfortable houses. Each member of the family had a particular role to play.

The father was the head of the household. He was often a stern figure, who was obeyed without question. While he went out to work every weekday, the mother looked after the house. In a middle class family, the children spent most of their time in the nursery, where they were brought up by a nanny. They might see their parents only once a day, before they went to bed. When the children grew up, only the sons were expected to work. They joined the army, or trained to be parsons, doctors, or lawyers. The daughters stayed at home with their mother. Their career was to get married as soon as possible.

Father – a doctor

Mother

Mistress (daughter)   Master

△ **A middle class family of the 1890s.**
● the mother would wear a fairly plain dress with lots of petticoats underneath
● the father wore a coat, close-fitting trousers, and white shirt with cravat collar
● the children wore similar clothes to their parents.

▷ **In the drawing room of a wealthy household in the 1880s.** This family has finished dinner. The butler is handing round a tray of drinks while a housemaid tends the fire. Many families would spend the evenings making their own kinds of entertainment, including:
● playing the piano and singing
● reading aloud from the latest novels or books of poetry
● playing cards, chess, or dominoes
● playing parlour games such as forfeits or charades
● playing billiards. (This was for the men only, as it gave them a chance to smoke their cigars.)

Between maid
Kitchen maid
Cook
Housemaid
Under Housemaid
Butler
Under Nurse
Footman
Gardener
Gardener's boy

Nurse
Coachman
Groom

△ **These are the servants** who worked for the family opposite. Each of them wears a uniform which suits their job. The housemaids and kitchen maids wear starched aprons. The butler wears a tie and the coachman wears a frock coat. The gardener and his boy wear corduroy trousers and waistcoats.

△ **A Victorian photograph showing father carving the joint of meat for Sunday lunch.** This was a solemn meal, especially for the children. They had to be well behaved at table, and only speak when a grown-up spoke to them. They also had to eat up all the food that was put on their plates.

All households, except the very poorest, had servants to do the daily work. Most important were the cook and the butler. The cook was in charge of shopping for food and running the kitchen, where she was helped by kitchen and scullery maids. The butler received visitors at the front door, and waited on the family of the house. Housemaids cleaned the rooms, while footmen did the heavier work, such as carrying coal and parcels.

Many young people came from the country to be servants in town houses. They felt lucky to have such good jobs, which gave them somewhere to live and clothes to wear. Being a servant was one of the few jobs a woman could find, apart from factory work. On average, they earned about £50 a year. They might spend all their working lives with the same household.

IN THE SUBURBS

By the 1860s, many industrial towns were overcrowded. The centres were clogged with shops, factories and busy streets. London alone contained nearly three million people. The only space for new housing lay in the countryside outside the towns.

The edges of towns were called the suburbs. At first, only the wealthy could afford to live so far from their workplaces. But public transport soon became cheaper and quicker. Regular horse-drawn bus services had begun in the 1830s. In 1863 the first London Underground Railway opened. Electric trams started running in big cities such as Leeds and Birmingham in the 1890s.

Now many people were able to move to the suburbs and commute to work each day. Huge areas of new housing were built. There was room for the houses to be larger than in the centres, with big gardens and wide roads between. Most were set together in terraces, though more expensive houses were separate, or detached.

△ Three blocks of flats built in Islington, London, in 1879. These were called New Model Dwellings, and were built to provide healthy and comfortable homes for working people. About 2,000 people lived in them. They paid a rent of just over 2 shillings (equivalent to about £7 at today's value) each week.

◁ **A baby's bath**, towels and can for carrying water. Very few houses had bathrooms or lavatories. Even Buckingham Palace had none when Victoria began her reign. Most people used outside lavatories, called privies. It was not until the end of the century that houses were supplied with running water from the mains.

24

▽ **A large suburban house in the 1880s.** It stands on the end of a terrace and has a glass conservatory. The house is built of red and grey bricks, with moulded bricks around the windows. The rooms are lit by gas and heated by coal fires. The coal is stored in a cellar under the house.

◁ **The street** is busy with tradesmen delivering goods to the houses. Letters are collected regularly from the pillar box, introduced in 1855.

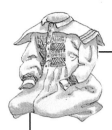

COUNTRY LIFE

During the 1850s there was a boom in farming. The new towns needed supplies of food. Grain and meat prices were high, and farmers could sell all they grew. But by 1875, the boom was over. Cheaper wheat began to flood in from the United States, and cheaper meat from Argentina and Australia. Food prices fell rapidly.

At the same time there was a series of bad harvests, and disease killed many cattle and sheep. Many farmers were ruined. But life was hardest for the farm labourers. There were now fewer jobs on the land than ever. New machines, such as steam threshers, saved time and needed few men to operate them.

△ **Victorian photograph of a ploughman** with his team of horses, taking a break from work. In 1850 the steam plough was invented, but it was not widely used for some years. It was hauled by steam engines.

△ **A squire with his family and servants** outside his country house at Ketteringham near Norwich in 1865. The servants of town houses were often not essential to the running of a home. But many people were needed to run country mansions and their vast estates. They included cooks, maids, gardeners, and gamekeepers. Some great houses had more than 100 servants.

▷ **Some of the main jobs on the farm in the 1880s:**

● Harvesting. The harvester (right) cut the corn with a sickle or scythe, which he kept very sharp. He could cut an area the size of a football pitch in a day.

● Haymaking. Women helped to turn the grass after it was mown (centre right) so that it would dry in the sun and wind. The hay was stored in tall stacks and fed to animals through the winter.

● Packing fruit and vegetables to take to market. (A market is shown far right.)

▽ **A steam-powered threshing machine at work.** The wheat was fed in and separated into grain and straw. Before this, threshing was done by hand. It was a long job which had earned the labourers much-needed extra money for winter.

The people who owned most of the land were very rich. A typical squire of the 1880s earned at least £3,000 a year from renting out land to farmers. But the people who worked on the land were very poor. Even in the 1880s, some farm labourers earned less than 10 shillings (50 pence) a week, with extra wages paid in beer, milk, or firewood.

Many workers rented their cottages from the farmer. The cottages were often very small, with only two rooms, and dark, damp, and draughty. If the worker lost his job, he would probably lose his home as well, and go to live in the parish workhouse. Some landowners looked after their labourers better. The Prince of Wales had over 70 new cottages built for his workers at Sandringham in Norfolk.

Many villagers kept a pig in their gardens, and grew vegetables. These were their chief source of food. Some got extra meat by poaching rabbits or pheasants from the squire's land. Any poacher who was caught would be fined or sent to prison.

After the slump of 1875, many workers moved to the towns, where they were better paid and worked shorter hours. In 1851, there were 1.3 million farmworkers. By 1901, there were only 0.7 million left.

EDUCATION

Until the 1840s, children did not have to go to school – and very few of them did. Even in 1861, a government report showed that of the population of 21 million there were only 2.5 million children at elementary (primary) schools. Many of these only went for less than a year, and few stayed on after the age of 10.

Education cost money. Wealthy people could afford to hire a governess or a tutor to teach their children at home. When they were older, the sons would be sent to stay (board) at a public school such as Eton or Rugby. The daughters were kept at home, and taught sewing, singing, and playing the piano.

Poor people also had to pay to send their children to school. Schools cost parents at least a penny a week for each child, and few working class families could afford this. The parents also needed the money the children could earn by working.

△ **A young boy sells matches in the street.** He is so poor that he has no shoes. Thousands of children never went to school at all, but worked on the streets to earn extra money for their families. Some sold flowers and fruit, and some swept roads.

Improved education
During Victoria's reign, schools were made better in many ways:
1840 The first teacher training college opens at Battersea in London.
1846 Clever pupils are used as teachers; some are only 10 years old.

1870 Education Act gives power to local school boards to start schools.
1880 Every child has to go to school between the ages of 5 and 10.

1891 Elementary education becomes free for all children.
1899 The school leaving age is raised to 12. Art and science are taught.

△ **A child scaring birds** from a wheat field with a rattle. There were many odd jobs which kept country children away from school. Some worked in field gangs, gathering stones, pulling turnips or stacking corn. The wages were vital to their families.

△ **A child sells newspapers.** As more people learned to read, newspapers became much more popular. In 1890, Britain's first daily newspaper with pictures, the *Daily Graphic*, was published.

▷ **Illustrated page from Dickens' *Oliver Twist*** (far right) showing Fagin, the organizer of child crime, in prison.

△ **Charles Dickens** was the most famous writer of the age. His novels included *Nicholas Nickleby*, which attacked the cruelty and bad conditions at cheap public (boarding) schools, and *Oliver Twist*, a tale of child thieves and poverty in London.

◁△ **Victorian classroom objects.** These included a handbell, Bible, and pupil's spectacles (far left), desk, slate and slate pencil (left), and writing books and ink pen (above).

There were several kinds of school for poorer children. The youngest might go to a Dame school, run by a local woman in a room of her house. The older ones went to a day school. There, the teacher was probably a local tradesman who made extra money by taking in pupils. Such schools were often dirty and very crowded.

Other schools were organized by churches and charities. Among these were the "ragged" schools, which were first set up in 1844 for orphans and very poor children. Schools like this had to be run very cheaply. They had few books apart from Bibles. Most of the teaching was done by monitors – older pupils who taught simple lessons to the younger ones.

School life was often very dull. Children were taught little apart from the "three Rs" – Reading, 'Riting and 'Rithmetic. They read aloud from books, which usually contained passages from the Bible. They wrote and did their sums, usually using chalk on slates.

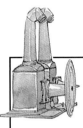

PASTIMES

By the second half of Victoria's reign, most people earned more money and worked shorter hours than ever before. For the first time, ordinary workers had enough leisure time to enjoy sports and other pastimes, and even to go away for holidays to the seaside.

△ **Cycling** became very popular. When the safety bicycle appeared in 1885, it was the cheapest way to travel. Townsfolk used bicycles to ride out into the countryside.

△ **Children play** in the street with an iron hoop. Most working class children spent their playtime out of doors, playing football, chasing games, or hopscotch.

▷ **Families pack into Terry's Theatre, London, in the 1880s** to watch a song-and-dance show. Places where people could go to be entertained included:
● **Theatres** Most large towns had several theatres.
● **Music halls** These were cheap and very popular.
● **Circuses** Circus companies toured the country.
● **Fairs** Most fairs took place on local holidays.

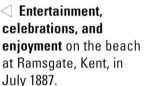

◁ **Entertainment, celebrations, and enjoyment** on the beach at Ramsgate, Kent, in July 1887.

Games such as football and cricket had been played for centuries. Now they were organized and given strict rules. The first FA (Football Association) Cup Final was played in 1871. During the 1880s, many of today's Football League clubs were established.

English and Australian teams played the first cricket Test Match in England in 1880. Among the players was W.G. Grace, the greatest sportsman of the age.

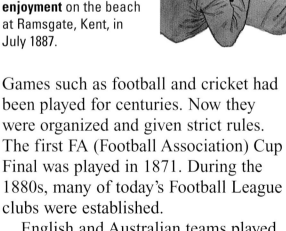

These organized matches soon drew large crowds. Watching had now become a pastime. But growing numbers also took part in new sports such as cycling, croquet, boating, or lawn tennis. During the 1870s, roller skating became a craze.

Meanwhile many old, crueller sports slowly disappeared. Bull-baiting had been banned by law in 1835. By 1849, cock-fighting was illegal too. But hangings were still public events until as late as 1868, and were always popular.

In 1871, the Bank Holiday Act declared that certain days throughout the year were official holidays (when banks and offices closed). The speed of railway transport meant that people could spend their days off at the seaside. Coastal towns such as Blackpool, Southend, Morecambe, and Brighton quickly grew into popular holiday resorts. In the cities, people could also enjoy the new parks, zoos, and museums.

▽ **Reconstruction of a Victorian nursery**. Girls in wealthy families had expensive toys such as rocking horses or doll's houses. Boys played with metal miniature soldiers or clockwork models. Poorer children bought their toys at penny bazaars. For one penny they could buy pencils, beads, tiny dolls, or tin badges.

MEDICINE AND SCIENCE

Diseases such as typhus and smallpox killed many thousands of Victorians. A lack of understanding about the main causes of ill-health led to many more people suffering. But, slowly, doctors and reformers made the nation healthier.

Improved health was partly because towns had cleaner water and better drains. It was also due to improvements in medicine. In the 1840s, surgeons began to use both anaesthetics to put patients to sleep for operations and antiseptics to stop infections. Children were vaccinated to prevent smallpox. Hospitals were kept clean to kill germs. Doctors and nurses were better trained.

Victorian scientists also made discoveries which helped people in other ways. Michael Faraday's experiments with electricity in the 1830s led to such inventions as the telegraph, the telephone, and the electric light. By the end of Victoria's reign, it was possible to take photographs, record sound, send messages using radio waves, and even drive a car.

Landmarks in Victorian science:
1839 William Fox Talbot makes photographic prints. William Cooke and Charles Wheatstone make the first railway telegraph.
1848 Lord Kelvin finds the lowest possible temperature: absolute zero (-273°C).
1859 Charles Darwin publishes his *Origin of Species*, stating that animal species evolve through natural selection.
1876 Alexander Graham Bell invents the telephone.
1879 Joseph Swan invents the electric light bulb.
1899 Guglielmo Marconi sends a wireless message across the Channel.

▷ **Science and society**
Right: Using an early telephone. The first exchange opened in 1878. Right centre: A box camera of about 1880. Photography became a popular hobby. Far right: Charles Darwin, whose revolutionary ideas on natural history caused a serious division between science and religion.

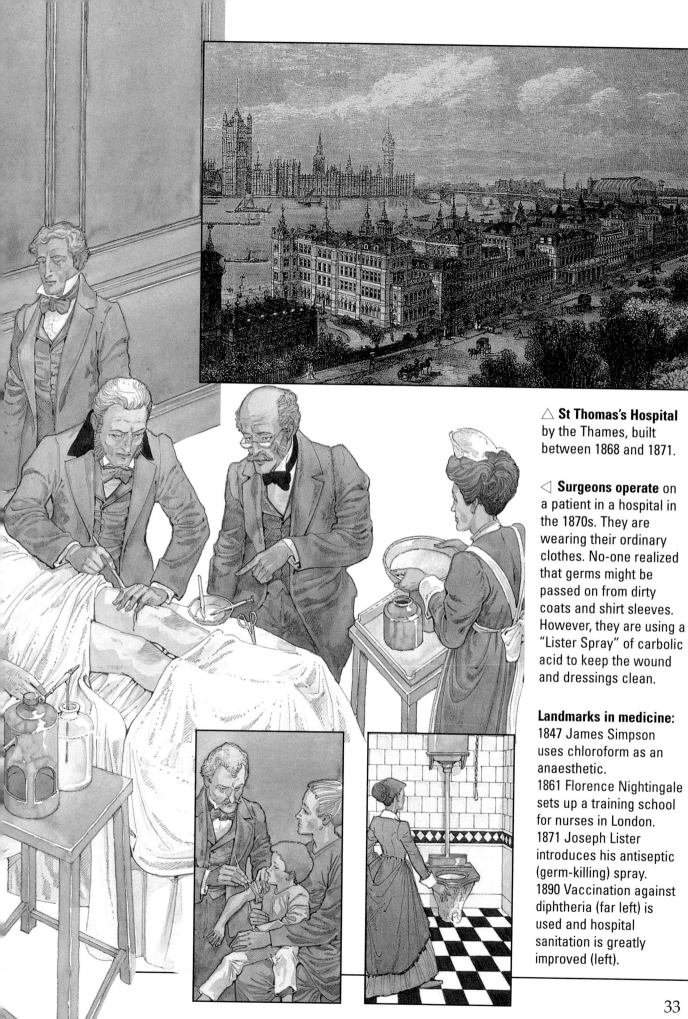

△ **St Thomas's Hospital** by the Thames, built between 1868 and 1871.

◁ **Surgeons operate** on a patient in a hospital in the 1870s. They are wearing their ordinary clothes. No-one realized that germs might be passed on from dirty coats and shirt sleeves. However, they are using a "Lister Spray" of carbolic acid to keep the wound and dressings clean.

Landmarks in medicine:
1847 James Simpson uses chloroform as an anaesthetic.
1861 Florence Nightingale sets up a training school for nurses in London.
1871 Joseph Lister introduces his antiseptic (germ-killing) spray.
1890 Vaccination against diphtheria (far left) is used and hospital sanitation is greatly improved (left).

WORKSHOP OF THE WORLD

British industry reached its peak in about 1890. In 1892, three out of every four new ships in the world were built in Britain. Cotton textiles, steel, machines, minerals, and coal were being sold as far away as Australia, India, and Canada.

The main raw materials for this success were coal and iron. New mining methods meant that more coal could be cut, and production shot up from 50 million tonnes in 1850 to over 150 million tonnes in 1890. With Henry Bessemer's invention of his converter in 1856, steel could at last be made from iron quickly and cheaply.

Steel was stronger and less brittle than iron, and many new uses were found for it. Railways were re-laid with steel track. Great steel bridges were built to carry the lines over wide rivers and estuaries. The biggest of these was the Forth Bridge, which was completed in 1890.

Steel also brought a great change to shipbuilding. It was lighter than iron, so bigger ships could be made. These new boats had propellers, powered by steam engines. Steam power began to take over from sail. In 1900, there were nearly as many steam ships as sailing ships.

Many important new uses were being found for steam. By the 1880s, steam engines were turning dynamos to make electricity in power stations. The electricity was used to drive factory machines. Then, in 1882, Joseph Swan set up generating stations. Soon, electric street lighting was introduced. Even some lighthouses had electric lights.

△ **Trial run on London's first** Underground Railway in 1863 between Paddington and the City.

▽ **An engineer's drawing** of 1880 for new street subways for sewers and pipes leading to shops and offices.

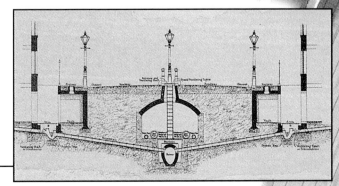

△ **Advert for a new type of dye** for sale in America, from about 1880.

Important advances in British industry:
1845 Alexander Parkes makes the first plastic from wood fibres.
1856 William Perkin makes a purple dye (aniline) from coal tar – the first artificial dye. Henry Bessemer invents the steel-converter.
1867 William Siemens invents an even more efficient open-hearth method of steelmaking.
1885 The railway tunnel is completed beneath the River Severn.
1890 Electric trains run on the London Underground. A power station first supplies electricity to the City.
1893 Ship Canal links Manchester docks with the sea.

◁ **A busy sea port** at the height of Britain's industrial age. Trains carry goods and passengers across a steel bridge. Steamships have been loaded with cargo bound for customers overseas.

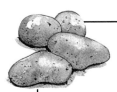

THE IRISH PROBLEM

By the 1840s, there were over eight million people in Ireland. At least half of them were poor peasants who rented tiny farms from landowners. Their main source of food was the potatoes they grew in their fields. But in 1845 this vital crop was destroyed by a disease called blight. In 1846, it struck Ireland again.

▷ **Policemen, bailiffs, and English soldiers** get ready to evict an Irish peasant farmer in 1850. Most peasants lived in huts like this, made of stones, sticks, and turf. The failure of the potato crop, and bad harvests of oats and barley, left the farmers with too little money to pay their rents. Between 1849 and 1852, more than 58,000 people were evicted and left homeless because they were behind on their rents. Some peasants fought back by burning ricks and threatening landowners.

The famine which followed was a calamity for Irish peasants. Nearly a million people died. Thousands more fled the country to find better conditions abroad. Between 1840 and 1860, two million Irish people emigrated to America. The British government was slow to give help. Worse still, it gave no protection to peasant farmers who were too poor to pay the rents on their land. Many were evicted from their homes by the landowners, most of whom lived in England.

The demand for Irish Home Rule grew stronger. In 1859, a secret society called the Fenian Brotherhood was formed. Its aim was to make Ireland independent, by force if necessary. They tried to seize Chester Castle in 1867, but were driven off. They also blew up a London prison, killing 12 people.

▷ **Irish emigrants wait at Liverpool docks** to board their ship to North America. Between 1800 and 1875, over 7.5 million people took this route. More than half of them were Irish. The early emigrant ships were powered by sail, and took seven weeks to cross the Atlantic. Poorer passengers were crammed together in steerage, below decks in the stern.

◁ **A cartoon of 1870 showing Gladstone** struggling with the problem of English landlords in Ireland. Gladstone became Prime Minister for the third time in 1886, and tried to have a Home Rule Bill passed by Parliament. But many in Gladstone's party (the Liberals) were against the Bill, and it was rejected. Gladstone's second Home Rule Bill of 1893 was defeated in the House of Lords.

△ **Charles Stewart Parnell** was a Protestant who became leader of the Irish Home Rule Party in 1877.

Unrest continued to grow in Ireland. Bands of men called Moonlighters attacked anyone who supported the English. A Home Rule Party was formed in 1870, and soon had 50 MPs. When Charles Stewart Parnell became its leader, he tried to get attention for its cause.

But the violence went on. In 1882, Irish terrorists murdered Lord Cavendish and his under-secretary in Phoenix Park, Dublin. Disgust at this turned many people against Home Rule. All the same, the Irish gained more seats in Parliament. The Prime Minister, William Gladstone, now supported the idea of Home Rule. But his first attempt to give Ireland its independence failed, and he was voted out of office. Then in 1890, Parnell was involved in a scandal over his affair with a married woman. The Home Rule Party dismissed him as leader.

Without Parnell, the party had no real voice in Parliament. When Gladstone tried a second Home Rule Bill, it was thrown out by the House of Lords. The Irish problem was far from being solved.

EXPLORERS AND MISSIONARIES

Many Victorian travellers set out for little-known parts of the world. Some went to trade, some to secure new territory for the British Empire. Missionaries, like David Livingstone, went to convert people to the Christian faith. But others went simply to explore, and to solve age-old mysteries.

Many of these mysteries lay in Africa. In 1857, John Hanning Speke set out to explore the great lakes of equatorial Africa. After several years he showed that the River Nile flowed out of a huge lake (which he named Lake Victoria). Other famous travellers came to the river. In 1864, Samuel Baker found a smaller lake further down the Nile (Lake Albert). And in 1875, Henry Morton Stanley sailed round Lake Victoria to prove that Speke had been right.

▽ **Victorian travellers in Africa took a mountain of equipment.** Here are some of the articles carried by porters on the expeditions of Speke, Baker and Stanley:
● rifles and pistols for hunting or protection from attack
● beads, silk cloth, blankets, cutlery and watches for presents or for trading
● an enamel bath
● a Persian carpet
● a wooden boat, made into five sections, which could be put together for sailing on Lake Victoria
● an iron chair
● tinned food from Fortnum & Mason store in London
● tents and other camping equipment
● medicine chests.

▽ **Speke and his party of native carriers** on the way to Lake Victoria.

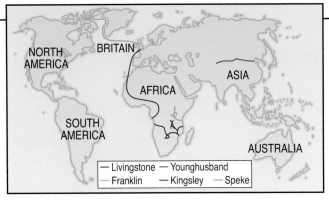

British explorers and where they went:
1848 Alfred Wallace and Henry Bates travel up the Amazon to Manaus.
1853 Richard Burton is the first white person to enter Mecca (in disguise).
1856 David Livingstone crosses Africa.
1860 Speke and Grant explore Lake Victoria.
1862 William Palgrave crosses Arabia.

1864 Samuel and Florence Baker reach Lake Albert in Africa.
1865 Edward Whymper climbs the highest peaks in the Andes.
1877 Stanley travels down the River Congo.
1891 Francis Younghusband crosses the Gobi Desert.
1893 Mary Kingsley travels in Angola and up the River Congo.

△ **Mary Kingsley** spent only a week in West Africa in 1897 but as a result she tried to change incorrect Victorian ideas about how Africans lived. She realized they might not need "civilising".

△ **Sir John Franklin** made several voyages to the Arctic. In 1845 he set out to find a sea passage north of America. His ships *Erebus* and *Terror* were caught in the ice, and the entire party perished.

Another mystery was the North-West Passage. For two centuries, sailors had tried to find a northerly route from the Atlantic to the Pacific. Franklin's expedition of 1845 disappeared into the icy wastes. No fewer than 40 rescue parties were sent from Britain to search for them, but it was not until 1857 that the bodies were found.

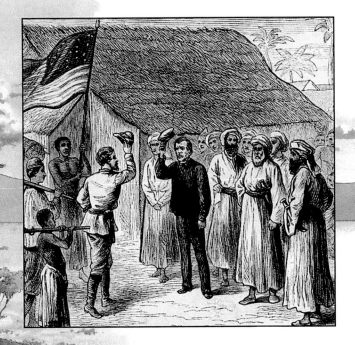

△ **Henry Stanley greets Livingstone at Ujiji, East Africa, in 1871.** People in Britain thought Livingstone was dead, and Stanley was sent out to find him.

Far to the south, two British travellers were exploring the River Amazon in South America. Henry Bates and Alfred Wallace were naturalists. In 1848, they took boats up the river, collecting specimens of the animals and plants.

An even more amazing journey was made by Sir Richard Burton in 1853. Disguised in Arab clothes, he became the first Westerner to enter the holy Muslim city of Mecca in Arabia.

THE BRITISH EMPIRE

"We hold a vaster empire than has been." These are the words on a Canadian stamp of 1898, showing a map of the British Empire. At its height, the empire covered one-fifth of the Earth's land surface, and contained over 370 million people.

Until about 1870, the empire had grown slowly. The British had gradually gained control of over half of India. Far Eastern ports in Singapore and Hong Kong had become important trading stations. Millions of settlers had emigrated to the wide open spaces of Canada, Australia, New Zealand, and South Africa.

The only way to reach the eastern part of the empire was by sea, around the southern tip of Africa. In 1869, the new Suez Canal opened a direct link between the Mediterranean Sea and the Indian Ocean. This made the voyage between India and Britain much quicker. In 1875, Benjamin Disraeli (then Prime Minister) bought enough shares in the canal to give Britain control of it. This increased British power in the East. During the 1880s, parts of Borneo, Burma, and New Guinea were added to the Empire.

Many men and much money were needed to control the growing British Empire. In 1893 the Army consisted of:
- 136,000 troops in Britain and Ireland
- 77,000 troops in India, supported by 160,000 Indian soldiers
- 47,000 troops in other territories, mainly South Africa and Egypt.

The Royal Navy had:
- 76,000 men
- 35 battleships
- 158 other warships.

▷ **The British Empire at its largest, in 1899.** The areas coloured red were under British control. They range from huge territories such as India, Canada, and Australia to important islands such as Hong Kong, Singapore, Jamaica, and Ceylon in the Indian Ocean.

Canada

India

Burma — Hong Kong

— Bahamas

— Gambia   Aden   British New Guinea

— Jamaica

British Guiana   Sierra Leone   Nigeria   British East Africa   Singapore

Gold Coast

Ceylon

South Africa   Australia

New Zealand

▷ **Singapore Harbour in the 1890s.** British residents take tea on deck. In the background is a Royal Naval gunboat, a symbol of British power. The island of Singapore was a major naval port, and a vital trading centre in South-East Asia. Rubber and other goods were shipped through here.

◁ **General Charles Gordon** at the fall of Khartoum in 1883. He was killed by followers of al-Mahdi, leader of a Muslim revolt.

By 1880 only one continent remained to be colonized: Africa. Here, Britain had to compete with other empire builders, especially France and Belgium. Each country grabbed land in what was called the "scramble for Africa". Within a few years, Britain took control of large parts of Africa, including Kenya, Uganda, Nigeria, and Egypt. British soldiers had to fight to hold on to these new territories. The bloodiest war took place in the Sudan in 1883, when rebels wiped out the British garrison at Khartoum.

▽ **Photograph of a tea plantation in India**, taken in 1876. British plantation managers oversee the work of local people.

END OF AN ERA

"To many of her people she is a name rather than a living reality." These were the words of *The Times* newspaper in 1887, when Victoria had been queen for 50 years. Since Albert's death in 1862 she had stayed in her palaces, and had rarely been seen by the public.

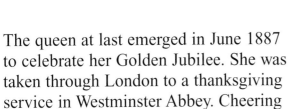

▷ **British troops wait for action during the Boer War.** The Boers were Dutch settlers in South Africa. In 1899 they rebelled against British rule. At first they had great success, defeating British armies three times during "Black Week". But the British slowly wore down Boer resistance, and they were forced to make peace in June 1902.

The queen at last emerged in June 1887 to celebrate her Golden Jubilee. She was taken through London to a thanksgiving service in Westminster Abbey. Cheering crowds lined the streets.

But the last years of the century were not all so happy. Britain was no longer the most important industrial nation in the world. She was challenged by the growing industrial power of the United States and Germany. Violence in Ireland was increasing, and 30 per cent of Londoners were living in great poverty.

There were also troubles overseas. It was costly and difficult to keep control of the massive empire. During Victoria's reign, 230 wars had been fought. Most had been small, but the 1890s saw major conflicts with the Boers and Afghans.

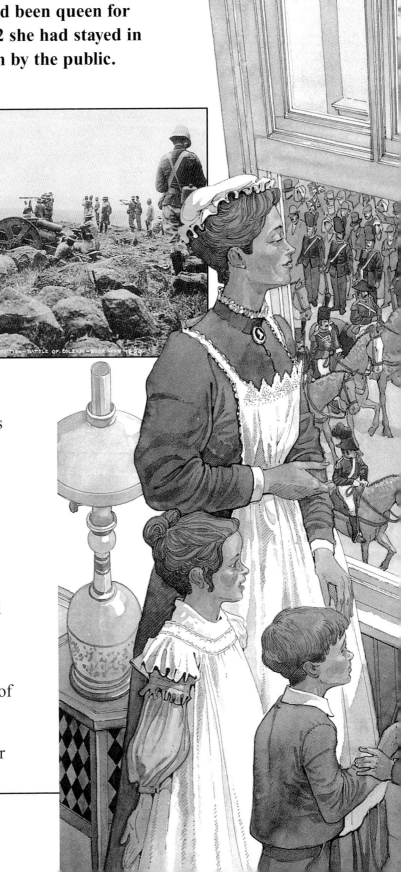

◁ **Queen Victoria with relatives from all over Europe.** The photograph, taken just a few years before Victoria died, includes Edward Albert, William II of Germany, and Czar Nicholas II of Russia. Edward Albert (known as 'Bertie') lived a very different kind of life from his strict and dignified mother. He enjoyed horseracing, gambling, sailing, and huge banquets. He bought an estate at Sandringham in Norfolk, where he shot many pheasants. The queen thought he was lazy, and would not allow him to do any important work. By the time she died in 1901, Edward was 59 years old.

◁ **A family watches** from an upstairs window as the queen passes by in her coach during her Diamond Jubilee in 1897. Some people paid over £2 for a good view of the procession.

Despite the troubles, there were even greater celebrations at Victoria's Diamond Jubilee in June 1897. Once again she rode through London. To escort her, there were 50,000 troops from all parts of the empire. Among them were Australian cavalrymen, camel riders from Africa, head-hunters from Borneo, and Indian princes. Royal Navy ships gathered at Spithead near Portsmouth on the south coast.

But by now the queen was an old woman. At the beginning of 1901 she was very weak. She died, aged 81, on 22 January. Her funeral was yet another grand state procession, but this time it marked the end of an era of British history. Victoria was buried beside Prince Albert at Windsor Castle.

FAMOUS PEOPLE OF VICTORIAN TIMES

Elizabeth Garrett Anderson, 1836–1917, was the first woman to become a doctor in Britain. She founded a hospital for poor women and children in London.

Isabella Beeton 1836–1865, was an English writer. Her *Book of Household Management* (1861) was a bestseller for many years.

Isabella Beeton

Isambard Kingdom Brunel, 1805–1859, was an engineer of many talents. He designed bridges, tunnels and steam ships (see page 11).

Richard Cobden, 1804–1865, was a Whig then Liberal MP. With John Bright, he founded the Anti-Corn Law League. He later opposed the Crimean War and campaigned for peace.

Charles Darwin, 1809–1882, was an English naturalist. He is famous for his theory of natural selection, which means that some animals are more able to survive than others. When published in 1859, this theory caused an uproar (see page 18).

Charles Dickens (1812–1870) was the greatest novelist of the age. His early novels, such as *Pickwick Papers,* are full of wonderful comic characters, but the later ones, for example *Bleak House,* are more gloomy (see page 29).

George Eliot was the pen-name of Mary Ann Evans, 1819–1880. She wrote several novels, including *Silas Marner* and *Middlemarch.*

William Gladstone, 1809–1898, was a Liberal politician and was Prime Minister four times. He was a deeply religious man who encouraged social reforms and tried to check the growth of the empire (see page 37).

W.G. Grace, 1848–1915, was an all-round cricketer. In his long career he broke many records and made the game widely popular (see page 30).

W.G. Grace

Thomas Hardy, 1840–1928, was an English novelist and poet. He was born in Dorset, and his stories were set in the Wessex countryside.

Octavia Hill, 1838–1912, worked for reforms of slum housing in London. She let houses to poor families for modest rents. She also helped to found the National Trust in 1895.

Mary Kingsley, 1862–1900, lived a quiet life at home until her parents died. Then, aged 30, she made two adventurous trips to West Africa. She gathered much information about African tribal customs (see page 39).

Joseph Lister, 1827–1912, was a Scottish surgeon. He realized the importance of keeping wounds and equipment germ-free during operations (see page 33).

David Livingstone, 1813–1873, was a missionary who made three long explorations of East Africa (see page 38).

William Lamb, Lord Melbourne, 1779–1848, was Victoria's first Prime Minister. She grew very fond of him, and he taught her the art of governing a country (see page 12).

Florence Nightingale, 1820–1910, was the founder of modern nursing. In 1854 she took charge of nursing soldiers wounded in the Crimean War (see page 16).

Henry John Temple, Lord Palmerston, 1784–1865, was a Whig then Liberal MP for over 50 years. He became Foreign Secretary in 1830 and Prime Minister in 1855 (see page 13).

Charles Stewart Parnell, 1846–1891, was an Irish political leader. He became an MP in 1875, and argued passionately for Irish independence (see page 37).

Robert Peel, 1788–1850, was twice Prime Minister. He was responsible for the repeal of the Corn Laws (see page 14).

Robert Gascoyne, Lord Salisbury 1830–1903, was Conservative Prime Minister during Victoria's last years.

Anthony Ashley Cooper, Earl of Shaftesbury, 1801–1885, was an upper-class landowner who did much to help the poor (see page 19).

Robert Louis Stevenson, 1850–1894, was a Scottish author. His books *Treasure Island* and *Kidnapped* are two of the most popular children's stories ever written.

Robert Louis Stevenson

Alfred, Lord Tennyson, 1809–1892, was the most famous Victorian poet. He wrote many poems about major events, such as the charge of the Light Brigade during the Crimean War.

ROYAL VICTORIANS FAMILY TREE

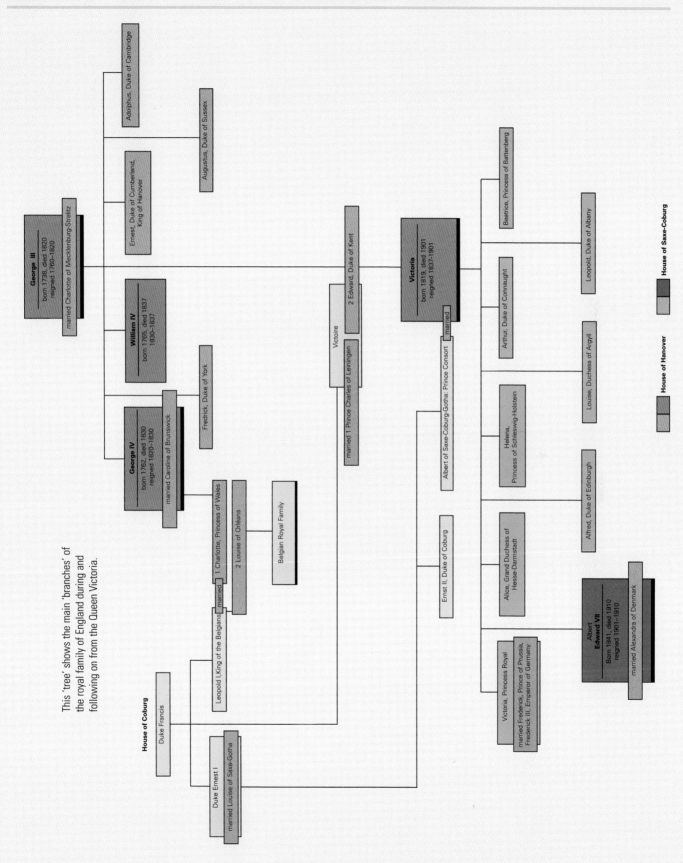

This 'tree' shows the main 'branches' of the royal family of England during and following on from the Queen Victoria.

House of Coburg

Duke Francis

Duke Ernest I — married Louise of Saxe-Gotha

Leopold I, King of the Belgians — married — 1 Charlotte, Princess of Wales / 2 Louise of Orléans

Belgian Royal Family

George III — born 1738, died 1820, reigned 1760–1820 — married Charlotte of Mecklenburg-Strelitz

Adolphus, Duke of Cambridge

Ernest, Duke of Cumberland, King of Hanover

Augustus, Duke of Sussex

William IV — born 1765, died 1837, 1830–1837

George IV — born 1762, died 1830, reigned 1820–1830 — married Caroline of Brunswick

Fredrick, Duke of York

Victoire — married 1 Prince Charles of Leiningen

2 Edward, Duke of Kent

Victoria — born 1819, died 1901, reigned 1837–1901 — married — Albert of Saxe-Coburg-Gotha: Prince Consort

Ernst II, Duke of Coburg

Beatrice, Princess of Battenberg

Arthur, Duke of Connaught

Leopold, Duke of Albany

Louise, Duchess of Argyll

Helena, Princess of Schleswig-Holstein

Alfred, Duke of Edinburgh

Alice, Grand Duchess of Hesse-Darmstadt

Victoria, Princess Royal — married Frederick, Prince of Prussia, Frederick III, Emperor of Germany

Albert Edward VII — Born 1841, died 1910, reigned 1901–1910 — married Alexandra of Denmark

House of Saxe-Coburg

House of Hanover

GLOSSARY

alliance agreement to work or fight together

ballot total of votes in an election

census official count and record of the population

colony land in which people from a foreign country settle and that is ruled from a distance by that country

commute live in a suburb, or out of town, and travel into the town to work each day

coronation ceremony of crowning a king or queen

evict force people to leave their home or land

evolution gradual change of something into a different form. Many Christians in Victorian times believed that animals could not evolve, but were exactly as they had been made by God.

flogging punishment in which the wrongdoer is whipped or beaten

foundry factory where metal ore is melted down, purified, and moulded

governess woman employed to teach and train children in a family

government people who run the country: the monarch, the Privy Council, Parliament and local officials

Home Rule freedom of a country to govern itself. This was the aim of Irish nationalists in the 1870s.

household people who work for or live with the owner of the house

Liberals one of the two main parties in Parliament. It grew out of the Whig party of the early 19th century, and encouraged reform and free trade.

missionary person who goes to do charitable or religious work in a foreign country.

music hall show consisting of short acts, such as singing, dancing, conjuring, and comedy.

mutiny uprising against the people in command. It is usually used to describe rebellions in the army and navy.

Parliament House of Lords (nobles and important churchmen) and the House of Commons (elected members) meeting to advise the monarch

safety bicycle bicycle with two wheels of the same size, driven by a chain. It was much safer than the old "Penny Farthing", which had one big and one small wheel. (A farthing was a small Victorian coin, value $\frac{1}{4}$ of an old penny.)

sewer underground drain for carrying away dirty water

slum area of crowded and squalid housing

suburb area of housing built on the edge of a town

tenement large building divided into separate flats for rent

textiles goods made from woven cloth

Tory one of the main parties in Parliament, which was to become the Conservative party. Most Tories opposed reform and supported the expansion of the empire.

tram type of bus which runs on rails and is powered by electricity

transportation punishment for a crime in which the prisoner was sent to work in a distant country, such as Australia

turbine machine containing a series of blades or buckets which are turned by the force of steam or water. Turbines are used to power engines or generate electricity.

vaccination injection of a person with a mild form of a disease. This builds up protection against that disease.

Whigs political party in Parliament which opposed the power of the monarch. It became better known as the Liberal party after the 1830s.

FIND OUT MORE

BOOKS

Access to History: The British Empire 1815–1914, Frank McDonough
(Hodder, 1994)

Real Lives: Victorian Town Children, Sallie Purkis (A & C Black, 2004)

Life in the Past: Victorian Homes, Mandy Ross (Heinemann Library, 2004)

People in the Past: Victorian Jobs, Brenda Williams (Heinemann Library, 2003)

You Wouldn't Want to Be: A Victorian Schoolchild, John Malam (Hodder, 2001)

WEBSITES

www.bbc.co.uk/history/lj/victorian_britainlj/preview.shtml
Interactive site about the Victorian period.

www.britishempire.co.uk
The history of the British Empire.

www.learningcurve.gov.uk/victorianbritain
Contains Victorian documents and other source material.

www.spartacus.schoolnet.co.uk
Wide-ranging site, including a feature on what it was like to be a child worker.

PLACES

Here are some museums and sites of Victorian interest to visit. Your local Tourist Office will be able to tell you about places in your area.

The Argory, County Tyrone, Northern Ireland   A Victorian house with a fascinating collection of furniture.

Buckingham Palace, London   Queen Victoria was the first to modernize this famous palace.

Calke Abbey, Derby   Hardly changed since the 19th century, it is full of everyday Victorian things.

Castle Museum, York   Includes a reconstruction of a Victorian parlour.

SS *Great Britain*, Bristol   Step back in time on board Brunel's SS *Great Britain* – the world's first large iron ship and the first to be driven by a screw propeller.

Highland Folk Museum, Kingussie, Scotland   Includes a copy of a turf-roofed hut lived in by 19th-century Scots.

Museum of Childhood, Edinburgh   Many Victorian toys and games can be seen in this museum.

National Railway Museum, York   A large collection of old steam railway engines and carriages.

North of England Open Air Museum, Beamish, County Durham   Among the many reconstructions are a Victorian school room and miner's cottage.

Welsh Industrial and Maritime Museum, Cardiff   Many relics of the industrial revolution.

INDEX

Act
  Education 28
  Factory 20
  Reform 5, 21
  Ten-Hour 20
Africa 41, 42
Albert, Prince 12, 13, 15
Alfred, Prince 13
Alice, Princess 13
Alton Towers 7
Anderson, Elizabeth
  Garrett 44
Anglicans 18
army 16, 21, 40
assassination attempt 13
Australia 26, 31, 34, 40

Baker, Samuel 38, 39
Balmoral Castle 13
Bates, Henry 39
bathrooms 24
battles
  Alma 16
  Balaclava 16
  Inkerman 16
  Sebastopol 16
  see also wars
Beeton, Isabella 44
Bell, Alexander Graham
  32
Bessemer, Henry 34
Boer War 42
bridges 11, 34
Bristol 10
Brunel, Isambard
  Kingdom 10, 11, 44
Burton, Sir Richard 39
bus services 24
butler 23

canals 9, 35
Carlyle, Thomas 12
Chadwick, Edwin 20
child labour 7, 20, 28, 29
chimney sweep 7
churches and chapels
  18–19
clothes 22
Cobden, Richard 44
coins 8,12
Corn Laws 14
coronation 12
country life 26–27
Crimean War 16–17
Crystal Palace 14
cycling 30

Darlington 10
Darwin, Charles 18, 32
Dickens, Charles 29, 44
diseases 9, 32
Disraeli, Benjamin 40

education 7, 28–29
Edward Albert, Edward VII
  13, 43
Eliot, George 44
emigration 36
Empire, British 16, 17,
  40–41,42
entertainment and
  pastimes 22, 30
Evangelicals 19
explorers 38, 39

factories 8–9, 10, 14, 20
family life 22–23
Faraday, Michael 32
farmers and farming 10,
  14, 26, 27, 36
Fenians 36
Franklin, Sir John 39
free trade 14

Gladstone, William 14, 37,
  44
Glasgow 8
Gordon, General Charles
  41
Grace, W.G. 31, 44
Great Exhibition 14, 15
Great Western ship 11
Great Western Railway
  10

Hardy, Thomas 44
health care 32, 33
Hill, Octavia 44
holidays 7, 31
Home Rule 37
hospitals 20, 32
houses and housing 8, 9,
  21, 24, 25

imports 14
India 17, 34, 40
industry 34–35
  see also factories,
  steam power
  inventions and science
  12, 32, 33
Ireland 10, 36, 42

Jubilee celebrations 42, 43

Kingsley, Mary 39, 44

lavatories 24
Law and order 21
Lehzen, Baroness 6
Lister, Joseph 33, 44
Liverpool 8, 9, 10, 15
Livingstone, David 38, 39
London 6, 8, 10, 12, 14,
  15, 19, 24, 30, 34, 42, 43

Lucknow 17

machinery, new types of
  8, 27
maids 23, 26
Manchester 8, 9,10
medicine 33
Melbourne, Lord 12, 13,
  44
middle class 22
Midlands, the 6, 7
mines and mining 9, 10, 20,
  34
missionaries 38–39
museums 12, 31
nanny 22

Natural History Museum,
  London 12
newspapers 29
Nightingale, Florence 16,
  33, 44

Palace
  Buckingham 13, 24
  Kensington 6
Palmerston, Lord 13, 44
Parliament and MPs 14, 19,
  37
Parnell, Charles Stewart
  37, 44
pastimes 30–31
Paxton, Joseph 14
Peel, Sir Robert 13, 14, 44
police force 14
poor people and
  peasants 7, 9, 18, 20, 27,
  36
potato blight 36
Prime Ministers 12, 37,
  44
Privy Council 12, 13
public school 28
public transport 24

railways 10, II, 14
religion 18–19
Royal Navy 40
Russia 16, 43

Salisbury, Lord 44
Salvation Army 20
Sandringham 27, 43
schools 28, 29
Scotland 9
servants 23, 26
Shaftesbury, Earl of 19, 20,
  44
Singapore 40
smoke from factories 6, 9
social reform 20–21

Speke, John Hanning 38,
  39
sports 31
squire 26, 27
stamps 12
Stanley, Henry Morton 38,
  39
steam power 10,14,15, 29,
  34
Stephenson, George 10,
  44
Stockton 10
suburbs 24–25
Sudan 40
Suez Canal 40
Sunday, as day of rest 18
Swan, Joseph 32, 34

tea plantation 41
telephone, early 32
Tennyson, Lord Alfred 44
theatres 30
Tories 12, 14
towns 8–9, 10
  see also houses and
  housing, suburbs
toys 31
trade 14–15
  see also industry
transport 10
transportation 21
tunnels 10, 35

Victoria 6–7,12–13, 18, 42,
  43

Wales 7, 19
  Prince of 27
Wallace, Alfred 39
wars 16
  see also specific wars
Watt, James 10
Wellington, Duke of 13,
  14
Whigs 12, 44
William IV 6, 12
Windsor Castle 13
workers and working
  class 7, 8, 9, 10, 18, 28